HISTORY & GEOGRAPHY 709
State Economics and Politics

LIFEPAC Test is located in the center of the booklet. Please remove before starting the unit.

Author:
Alpha Omega Staff

Editor:
Alan Christopherson, M.S.

Westover Studios Design Team:
Phillip Pettet, Creative Lead
Teresa Davis, DTP Lead
Nick Castro
Andi Graham
Jerry Wingo

804 N. 2nd Ave. E.
Rock Rapids, IA 51246-1759

State Economics and Politics

Introduction

We are all citizens of one state or another. Each of the fifty states of the Union has a government. As citizens of those fifty states we should try to understand as much as possible the workings of those state governments. This LIFEPAC® is designed to serve that end. Since all the states are different from one another, only a general coverage is practical here. We can, however, study this material and acquire a better knowledge of the particular state in which we live. Let us prayerfully consider our duties as Christian citizens. Let us seek to learn the facts contained herein so that we may better serve our country and our God.

Objectives

Read these objectives. The objectives tell you what you will be able to do when you have successfully completed this LIFEPAC. When you have finished this LIFEPAC, you should be able to:

1. Explain the background of state government.

2. Describe the structure of state government.

3. Discuss the significance of state spending.

4. Enumerate the types and meaning of state taxes.

5. Relate to taxes as a Christian citizen.

6. Explain and evaluate state borrowing.

7. Describe state political parties.

8. Differentiate between liberals and conservatives.

9. Discuss the elements of political power.

Survey the LIFEPAC. Ask yourself some questions about this study and write your questions here.

_____

_____

_____

_____

_____

_____

_____

_____

_____

_____

_____

_____

_____

_____

_____

_____

_____

_____

_____

1. STATE GOVERNMENT

In this section we shall consider the background and structure of state government. By background we mean the history of how states came to be and how they came to have the kind of government we find in the United States of America.

By structure we mean the way in which the various states have set up their governing bodies. This discussion should give us a better understanding of how state government works.

SECTION OBJECTIVES

Review these objectives. When you have completed this section, you should be able to:

1. Explain the background of state government.
2. Describe the structure of state government.

VOCABULARY

Study these words to enhance your learning success in this section.

bill (bil). A proposed law presented to a lawmaking body for its approval.

confederacy (kun fed' ur u sē). A union of countries or states.

derive (di rī v'). Obtain from a source; get; receive.

nullification (nul u fu kā' shun). The act of making null; canceling; voiding.

ratify (rat' u fī). To confirm; approve.

sovereign (sov' run). Independent of the control of another government.

Note: *All vocabulary words in this LIFEPAC appear in* **boldface** *print the first time they are used. If you are not sure of the meaning when you are reading, study the definitions given.*

Pronunciation Key: h**a**t, **ā**ge, c**ã**re, f**ä**r; l**e**t, **ē**qual, t**ė**rm; **i**t, **ī**ce; h**o**t, **ō**pen, **ô**rder; **oi**l; **ou**t; c**u**p, p**u̇**t, r**ü**le; **ch**ild; lo**ng**; **th**in; /FH/ for **th**en; /zh/ for mea**s**ure; /u/ or /ə/ represents /a/ in **a**bout, /e/ in tak**e**n, /i/ in penc**i**l, /o/ in lem**o**n, and /u/ in circ**u**s.

BACKGROUND

The basic political unit in the United States is the state. The state has a unique function in the American system of government because of the way the nation developed. Remember that thirteen independent colonies united in a relatively loose organization or **confederacy** to fight the British. After victory was secured, the purpose of this union had been served. Each colony was a **sovereign** entity again. They were really thirteen separate countries.

At the end of the war, a very weak government was set up based upon what were called the *Articles of Confederation.* This government was basically a continuation of the old Continental Congress that had led the war for independence. The former colonies retained most of their independent character.

The situation was quite awkward. Congress could not collect taxes but had to ask the states for money. The Articles of Confederation were really more of a treaty between sovereign, independent states than of a unified government.

| Independence Hall – Birthplace of the Constitution

The Constitution was drafted in an effort to strengthen the national government. In fact, the original purpose of what is now called the Constitutional Convention was to revise the Articles, not to draft a new document. The drafting of a new Constitution was a radical departure from the legal purpose of the Convention. That fact is probably one reason that the deliberations were held behind closed doors.

The new *United States Constitution* was signed in 1787 and was completely **ratified** in 1790. The last state to ratify was Rhode Island. It did so on May 29, 1790.

Although the present Constitution greatly expands the power of the federal government, its assumption is that all powers not given to the national government belong to the states or to the people. Federal authority is conceived of as a **derived** authority. The national government is the United States government.

However, its authority and power to exist are derived from the authority already held by the states themselves. The derived nature of federal authority is the reason that state governments look upon themselves as being independent of the national government.

One of the major issues of United States history has been the rightful extent of federal authority and whether the states are allowed to oppose unlawful extensions of federal power. War was declared in 1812 between the United States and England. Most New England federalists opposed the war. Several New England states refused to participate in any way other than by mounting a defense against invasion. The General Assembly of Connecticut in the Connecticut Resolves declared "that the State of Connecticut is a Free, Sovereign, and Independent state; that the United States are a confederacy of States; that we are a confederated and not a consolidated Republic." The legislators wanted their independence from the national government.

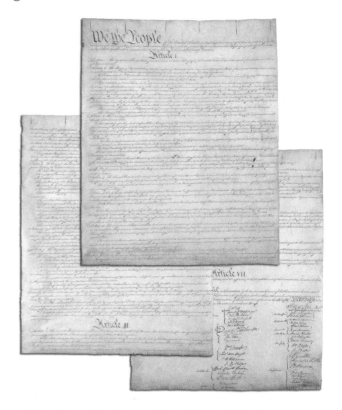

| The Constitution of the United States

Several New England states also opposed the Embargo Act of 1814, which sought to stop all shipping and other commercial activity in United States waters. The legislatures of these states refused to comply with the federal law. They were using the principle of *interposition*. By this term is meant the use of state sovereignty to block enforcement of a federal law that the state considers unconstitutional. The state interposes its authority over that of the federal government.

The principle was first set forth in the Virginia Resolution of 1798:

"That this Assembly doth explicitly and peremptorily declare, that it views the powers of the federal government, as resulting from the compact, to which the states are parties, as limited by the plain sense and intention of the instrument constituting that compact; as no further valid than they are authorized by the grants enunciated in that compact; and that in case of a deliberate, palpable, and dangerous exercise of other powers, not granted by the said compact, the States who are parties thereto, have the right, and are in duty bound, to interpose for arresting the progress of the evil, and for maintaining within their respective limits, the authorities, rights, and liberties appertaining to them."

Ironically, the author of the Virginia Resolution was James Madison. During his presidency the New England states would invoke the doctrine of interposition against federal measures related to the War of 1812.

An extension of the principle of interposition was **nullification**. This term meant that a state could declare a federal law null and void within its borders. Although the New England states had also used this principle at the time of the War of 1812, nullification was chiefly associated with the views of John C. Calhoun, a senator from South Carolina.

He wrote:

"The right of interposition, thus solemnly asserted by the state of Virginia, be it called what it may—State-right, veto, nullification, or by any other name—I conceive to be the fundamental principle of our system, resting on facts historically as certain as our revolution itself, and deductions as simple and demonstrative as that of any political or moral truth whatever; and I firmly believe that on its recognition depend the stability and safety of our political institutions..."

Eventually, Southerners who believed as Calhoun did would accept the doctrine of *secession* which said that a state had the right to leave the Union if it thought that the Union had violated its rights. Others disagreed, saying no state could disobey a federal law, much less break the Union. The issue was settled in blood. The Civil War was won by the Union and the door was closed to secession. This war created no legal solution to the problem; the question was simply eliminated by force.

However, the issue of state sovereignty remains, even though no one talks of secession. How sovereign are the states? What is the legitimate extent of federal authority? The question is now largely left to the courts, which consider each issue separately. The trend has been a diminishing of state sovereignty and an increase in federal power.

This increase in federal power at the expense of the state does not mean that state sovereignty does not exist today. State governments are still pursuing their own courses. They do not consult with Washington concerning actions. States' rights, though diminished, are still with us and play a large role in shaping the character of the United States system.

One cannot understand either state government or federal government without a basic comprehension of the original sovereignty of the state governments and the derived sovereignty of the national government. This system of government is unique to the United States.

The term *state* can mean several things. It may refer to general conditions in a certain context. For example, "the state of the weather" or "the state of the roads." It may be used as a synonym for government or the body politic. Some will speak of the growth of state power or the extension of the state into every area of life; in these cases, what is meant is the government in general.

For the purposes of this LIFEPAC, the term *state* refers to the basic units of United States government. A state is roughly similar to the provinces that compose some other countries, but it differs from them because of the historical background we have just discussed. The United States is composed of fifty states. The reason that the state is referred to as the basic unit of government is twofold. First, the United States government derives its authority from the states. This assumption implies that the states have a built-in sovereignty. Second, the state government is the creator of all other levels of government. It is, therefore, the central unit.

The following map is a map of the fifty states. Can you find your state? What is the name of your state? What states border your state?

| The United States of America

Match the terms.

1.1	_____ bill	a. obtain from a source; get; receive
1.2	_____ confederacy	b. a union of countries or states
1.3	_____ derive	c. independent of the control of another government
1.4	_____ nullification	d. the act of making null; canceling; voiding
1.5	_____ ratify	e. to confirm; approve
1.6	_____ sovereign	f. a proposed law presented to a lawmaking body for its approval

Write the letter for the correct answer on the line.

1.7 The basic political unit in America is the _____ .
   a. federal government   b. democracy
   c. county   d. state

1.8 How many independent colonies did the United States originally have when they banded together to fight the British? _____
   a. fifty   b. thirteen   c. five   d. sixteen

1.9 The Articles of Confederation were basically a continuation of the _____ .
   a. revolutionary army   b. Continental Congress
   c. English Parliament

1.10 Under the Articles of Confederation, Congress could not collect its own _____ .
   a. taxes   b. laws   c. statutes   d. amendments

1.11 Rather than a government, the Articles were more like a _____ .
   a. club   b. state   c. treaty   d. right-to-work law

1.12 The Constitution was drafted in an effort to strengthen the _____ .
   a. state government   b. national government
   c. regional government   d. county government

1.13 The original purpose of the Constitutional Convention was to _____ .
   a. revise the Articles of Confederation   b. write a new Constitution
   c. elect a president   d. none of the above

1.14 The Constitution was signed in _____ .
   a. 1885   b. 1776   c. 1787   d. 1607

1.15 The Constitution assumes that all powers not specifically granted to the national government are retained by the people or the _____ .

    a. Congress   b. counties   c. states   d. Supreme Court

1.16 Federal authority is _____ .

    a. sovereign authority   b. derived authority

    c. complete authority   d. weak authority

1.17 American state governments possess a sovereignty _____ .

    a. independent of the federal government   b. inferior to the federal government

    c. equal to that of the federal government

1.18 In which war did some of the New England states refused to participate _____ in any way other than mounting a defense against invasion? _____

    a. the American Revolution   b. the Civil War

    c. World War II   d. the War of 1812

1.19 "The use of state sovereignty to block enforcement of a federal law that the state considers unconstitutional" is the definition of _____ .

    a. veto   b. interposition   c. secession   d. entreaty

1.20 The doctrine of interposition was first enunciated in the _____ .

    a. Connecticut Resolves of 1798   b. Texas Observer of 1798

    c. Virginia Resolution of 1798

1.21 The doctrine of nullification was associated with _____ .

    a. Calvin   b. Knox   c. Wesley   d. Calhoun

1.22 The option of a state's seceding from the Union was closed by the _____ .

    a. apostolic succession   b. Civil war

    c. Emancipation Proclamation

1.23 Has the sovereignty of the states increased? _____

    a. yes   b. no

Complete these activities.

1.24 The number of states in the United States is _____ .

1.25 Name two reasons that the state is called the basic unit of our government.

    a. _____

       _____

    b. _____

       _____

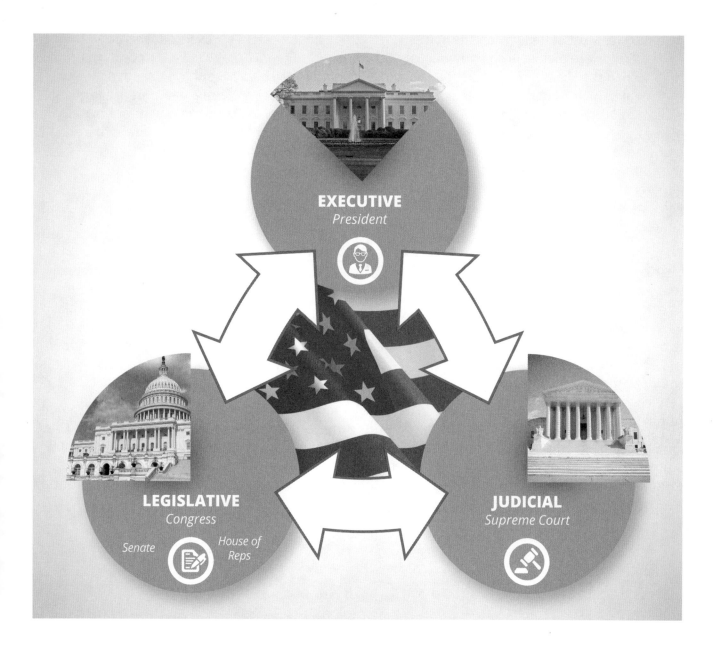

STRUCTURE

State government, like the federal government, is divided into three branches: the *legislative,* the *executive,* and the *judicial.* These three branches are designed to provide checks and balances upon one another. The men who founded the United States system of government were very wise. They agreed with Lord Acton, "All power tends to corrupt, and absolute power corrupts absolutely." Their object was to limit the power of any one person or institution.

The leaders of the original thirteen states borrowed many ideas from Montesquieu, a French philosopher who recommended the system of checks and balances in his *Spirit of the Laws.* This book was widely read in colonial times–especially by men such as Adams, Jefferson, and Madison.

Legislative. Most state legislatures in the United States are divided into two houses, normally called the House of Representatives and the Senate. Such a legislature with two houses is termed *bicameral.* The state of Nebraska has a one-house legislature. It is termed *unicameral.* The lawmaking body is not always termed the state legislature. It can also be called the general assembly (as it is in nine states), the legislative assembly (in three states), or the general court (in two states).

The state House of Representatives is presided over by the *Speaker of the House*, who is normally elected by the members at the beginning of each session. Houses of Representatives vary in size from up to four hundred members to as few as thirty-five. The average state House of Representatives, however, has about one hundred members. These members are chosen from throughout the state on the basis of population.

One problem traditionally has been that some state legislatures do not have equal representation. Usually the rural population has been over-represented, and the urban population has been under-represented. This condition reflects the fact that we were once a predominantly agricultural country. Recent actions by the United States Supreme Court are tending to correct these imbalances so that both city citizens and suburban citizens are more equally represented.

Another trend is to *single-member* districts. In some states some counties or legislative districts have been represented by *at-large* members. At-large representatives are elected by all the voters in the area. The result can be that a group of voters (such as suburbanites) dominate the election, and poorer areas are often under-represented. To counteract this tendency, districts have been divided into smaller geographical units. As a result, more people from minority groups now serve in state legislatures.

The *Speaker of the House* often wields a tremendous amount of authority. They are often able to appoint committee chairmen and to control what legislation will be considered. Of course, the speaker also decides who may speak out on the legislature floor.

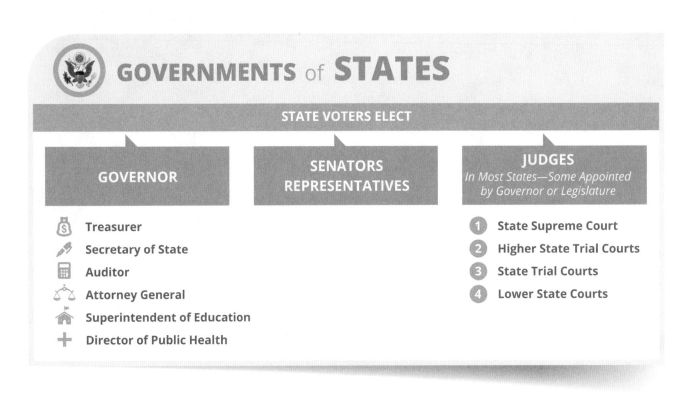

GOVERNMENTS of STATES

STATE VOTERS ELECT

GOVERNOR

SENATORS REPRESENTATIVES

JUDGES
In Most States—Some Appointed by Governor or Legislature

- Treasurer
- Secretary of State
- Auditor
- Attorney General
- Superintendent of Education
- Director of Public Health

1. State Supreme Court
2. Higher State Trial Courts
3. State Trial Courts
4. Lower State Courts

Not all state legislatures are divided into two parties. Some states (such as Nebraska) do not have party politics as part of the legislative election. Some legislatures are almost totally dominated by one party. Traditionally most southern state legislatures have been composed almost completely of Democrats. In some Western states, the Republican party has been in a similar position. This situation is beginning to change. In no-party legislatures or in one-party legislatures, divisions tend to be along *liberal* versus *conservative* lines. Liberals are those who tend to favor more government programs, bigger budgets, and increased social legislation. Conservatives are those who support less government, balanced budgets, and private solutions to human problems.

The majority party controls the legislature. The speaker is chosen from, and by, the majority party. Both parties elect floor leaders; therefore, the legislature has both a majority leader and a minority leader. Committee chairmen are from the majority party.

The state Senate (or upper house) is smaller than the House of Representatives. Senators represent broader segments of the population. The Senate is presided over by the lieutenant governor, normally chosen in a popular election. Senators often serve for longer terms than representatives.

Many state legislatures meet *biennially,* that is, once every two years. Sometimes the sessions are limited to a certain number of days (60 or 120, for example), after which the legislature can only meet at special sessions called by the governor. Other state legislatures meet every year.

Thousands of **bills** are proposed at each legislative session. Most do not pass; some are not even considered.

The following steps indicate the progress of a bill through the legislature:

1. The bill is introduced. Usually it is placed in some kind of container (often called the "hopper").

2. The bill is given a number, and the speaker of the house assigns it to a committee.

3. The committee considers the bill. Committee chairmen normally control which bills will actually be discussed.

4. The bill is either rejected by the committee or reported out of committee. In other words, the bill is sent to the floor of the House for debate and approval. By this time the original bill may have several amendments.

5. The bill is argued and voted on by the lower House. If the bill passes the lower House, it is sent on to the Senate. Of course, bills may also originate in the Senate and be sent on to the lower House.

6. The Senate also has committees, and a Senate committee now considers the bill. If it is accepted, the bill goes to the Senate floor for approval or rejection.

7. Often the Senate and House versions of the same bill are different. The senators may have included some items of which the House did not approve or vice versa. Therefore, the bill is sent to a conference committee composed of members of both houses. Here, the differences are ironed out.

8. After the conference committee has composed a bill that appears acceptable to both houses, the bill is returned to both houses for a vote. If they pass the same bill, it is sent to the governor.

9. The governor then either signs the bill into law or vetoes (rejects) it. One way to veto a bill is called the *pocket veto*. The governor simply puts the bill away, or "pockets" it, until the session is over so that the legislature will not be able to override the veto.

10. Normally, the legislature can override the governor's veto if at least two-thirds (or occasionally three-fourths) of the members favor the bill.

When a committee of the legislature is considering a bill, it hears from those citizens who favor or oppose the proposed legislation. Those who testify before the committee may be bureaucrats from the state government, businessmen who will be affected by the law, or other interested citizens.

Some organizations keep full-time personnel at the state capitol. These people are paid to work with and influence the legislature. They talk to individual legislators about bills that are about to be introduced, they testify before committees, and they keep the group they represent informed about upcoming legislation. Men or women who do this kind of work are called *lobbyists*. Sometimes the groups they represent are called *special interest groups*.

Lobbyists may represent teachers, insurance companies, utilities, real estate brokers, day care centers, consumer groups, retired people, unions, or just about any other kind of group.

Special interest groups are really just citizens who share a common cause or occupation.

In some cases, lobbyists have attempted to bribe legislators with money or other gifts, and sometimes they have succeeded. Most lobbyists are channels of information to the members of the legislature and to those they represent.

Complete these activities.

1.26 What are the three main branches of the state government?

a. _____

b. _____

c. _____

1.27 What are the three branches designed to do?

_____

1.28 What did Lord Acton say about power?

_____

_____

1.29 The author whose thought provided theoretical justification for the organization of the U.S. government was a. _____ , and his book was called the b. _____ of the c. _____ .

1.30 What is the difference between a bicameral and unicameral legislature?

_____

_____

1.31 What are the two houses of a state legislature usually called?

a. _____

b. _____

1.32 The a. _____ of the house usually presides over the lower legislative house while the b. _____ presides over the upper.

1.33 On what basis are representatives distributed throughout the state? _____

Complete these sentences.

1.34 One traditional problem of state legislatures has been that rural districts have been

a. _____ while urban areas have been

b. _____ .

1.35 A state legislature that meets biennially meets every _____ years.

1.36 Those who tend to be in favor of less government and balanced budgets are called

_____ .

1.37 The member of a state legislature who controls what legislation will be considered and decides who may speak on the floor is the a. _____ of the b. _____ .

1.38 State governments, like the federal government, are divided into _____ branches.

1.39 The only state with a one-house legislature is the state of _____ .

1.40 One difference between political liberals and conservatives is that _____ tend to favor a balanced budget.

1.41 The legislature in a two-party state is controlled by the _____ party.

1.42 In state legislatures the a. _____ is larger than the b. _____ .

1.43 A session called by the governor to consider legislation when the legislature does not normally meet is called a _____ session.

1.44 As a result of dividing districts into smaller geographical units, more people from _____ groups now serve in state legislatures.

1.45 Representatives of special-interest groups who attempt to persuade legislators to pass certain bills are known as _____ .

1.46 Citizens with a common cause or occupation are members of _____ groups.

Complete this activity.

1.47 List the ten steps through which a bill progresses in the legislature. Assume it starts in the House of Representatives.

a. _____

b. _____

c. _____

d. _____

e. _____

f. _____

g. _____

h. _____

i. _____

j. _____

Executive. The executive branch of the state government is headed by the *governor,* but it includes a host of departments and agencies. Some of these departments are dependent on the governor and some are not.

The power of the governor varies from state to state. In some states (notably, Illinois, New York, and California) the governor has strong executive powers. They are is actually the chief administrator to whom most other administrators report.

In many other states this situation does not exist. The governor has weak powers, and executive power is spread among several elected officials and even some boards and commissions. Weak governorships are characteristic of Southern and border states where the bitterness brought on by Reconstruction governors following the Civil War resulted in the adoption of the long ballot, in which almost every major officeholder is elected.

Even in states with a strong governor, the attorney general is always elected. Other states also elect the state secretary, state treasurer, state auditor, and lieutenant governor.

If the governor's cabinet is composed of their own appointees, the governor is stronger than a governor whose cabinet is elected. Elected officials do not feel a responsibility to the chief executive; their responsibility is to the people, to the voters who elected them. A governor can only influence such people through a persuasive personality, by a logical argument, or through the dignity of the governor's office. They have more influence if the other officials are from the same political party than if they are not.

Many states not only have the public officials just mentioned, but they also have a number of boards and commissions. These bodies may be elected, or they may be appointed. They tend to be more responsible to the legislature than to the governor.

- Controls state police & national guard
- Coordinates civil defense
- Prepares budgets
- Appoints judges
- Vetoes legislation
- Calls special sessions of the legislature
- Pardons criminals
- Commutes sentences
- Acts as head of their political party

Governor's Duties

The reason for the scattering of executive responsibility is the long-cherished belief in the freedom of the individual as well as the lack of freedom found in concentrations of power. People in the United States have always avoided the placing of a few men in positions of great authority.

The argument against the long ballot and a weak governor is that it results in a weak and inefficient administration. Some people believe that concentration of power would make the management of government more effective. This point is debatable. Surely many overlaps of responsibilities and administrative bottlenecks occur because of the scattering of executive power, but the various semi-independent departments and agencies also act as a check and balance system and curb each other's power. Many a Southern state or Midwestern state with a weak governor is in a better social and financial position than New York and California, which have stronger governors and a more highly centralized administration.

All governors have a similar set of administrative responsibilities. Often they control the state police. They direct the national guard (or state militia) unless it is in the federal service. They are usually in charge of coordinating civil defense efforts. Governors prepare state budgets, appoint magistrates and judges (at least those who are not elected), appoint replacements to unexpired terms of elected officials (United States senators, commission members, judges, and so on), and veto legislation.

Some governors have the "item veto" in which the governor has the power to veto part of a bill and not all of it. The governor's budget is submitted to the legislature at the beginning of each regular session. The lawmakers then spend most of the session considering and amending it. The governors of most states may call a special session of the legislature if they believe that a certain type of legislation is still needed.

One of the most awesome powers of the governor is that of *pardon.* The governor may pardon a criminal and, as a result, free them from the sentence of a court. This power applies to those accused of murder and awaiting capital punishment as well as to ordinary criminals. The governor may also *commute* a sentence; they may lessen the time the prisoner must serve or change the type of punishment. For example, a man sentenced to 30 years in prison may have their time shortened to 10 years.

The governor is usually the official or actual head of their party. This is not always the case, however. Sometimes an influential senator or representative may also have a significant following in the party. If several cabinet officials

- Presides over state senate
- Acts as a member of boards and commissions
- Fills in for governor if necessary

Lieutenant Governor's Duties

are elected, these men may be eyeing the governor's office as a future career.

The *lieutenant governor* presides over the state senate and is often quite powerful in their role. Like the Speaker of the House, the lieutenant governor has a significant amount of authority over committee assignments and over the flow of legislation. They also may in some states be a member of several boards and commissions in the executive branch. Normally, the lieutenant governor steps up and completes the governor's term if the governor should die in office, resign, or be removed.

Another very powerful state official is the *attorney general.* They are the state's lawyer, and they represent the state in court. The attorney general gives legal opinions to the legislature, to government agencies, or to the local governments when such advice is sought. They are particularly sought after on matters involving the state constitution. The attorney general does not normally prosecute criminal and civil cases; this type of work is usually done at the local level by a district attorney. Often, they are empowered to investigate and prosecute vice operations and organized crime within the state. Usually, the state attorney general is an elected official. They may sometimes embarrass the governor politically by investigating corruption in the executive branch.

The *secretary of state* is the keeper of the state seal. They issue certificates of incorporation, oversee the state archives (public documents and the place where they are kept), direct elections, publish all state laws, and may even issue license plates.

The *state treasurer* administers state funds, invests them, distributes them to state agencies, and may even be responsible for collecting taxes.

The *state auditor* approves all payment of bills by the state and also audits (analyzes financially) all the various departments and agencies of the state government. This acts as a check upon dishonesty in the use of state funds.

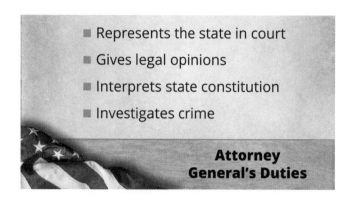

- Represents the state in court
- Gives legal opinions
- Interprets state constitution
- Investigates crime

Attorney General's Duties

States may also appoint or elect a superintendent of public instruction. They work with the state school board in overseeing the state school system.

Normally, a host of regulatory agencies and commissions exist within the state government. The state utilities commission sets rates that public utilities (telephone companies, electric utilities, and gas companies) may charge. The state insurance board or commission regulates the insurance business. The oil and railroad commissions regulate those businesses. The state welfare department may distribute funds to the needy, provide hospitals for the handicapped, regulate and investigate child abuse, and control the day care industry.

Sometimes these agencies have powers that are far more extensive than executive powers. They may have quasi-legislative (seemingly legislative) and quasi-judicial (seemingly judicial) powers. They may issue orders that have the force of law, and they may also be the court that enforces these orders. The field of administrative law is one that has dangers for individual liberty. It removes the lawmaking and judicial functions from constitutional and political safeguards.

✎ **Complete these sentences.**

1.48 The _____ branch of state government is headed by the governor and includes a number of departments and agencies.

1.49 The power of the chief executive, the _____ , varies from state to state.

1.50 Illinois, New York, and California have a a. _____ governor, but many Southern and border states have a b. _____ governor.

1.51 Many Southern states have the _____ ballot, in which almost every major official is elected.

1.52 Normally if a governor dies in office, they are replaced by the _____ .

1.53 The governor whose cabinet is composed of their own appointees is stronger than the one whose cabinet is _____ .

1.54 The scattering of executive power in the United States reflects the long-cherished belief in the _____ of the individual and the lack of freedom in concentrations of power.

1.55 Those who oppose the long ballot insist that it results in a weak and inefficient _____ .

1.56 In a state with a weak governor, the various semi-independent departments and agencies act as a a. _____ and b. _____ system and curb each other's power.

1.57 Governors head the state _____ and the national guard.

1.58 Governors are charged with coordinating _____ defense efforts.

1.59 The governor prepares the state a. _____ , appoints judges, appoints replacements to unexpired terms of elected officials, and b. _____ legislation they do not like.

1.60 The power to veto part of a bill is called the _____ veto.

1.61 The governor of most states may call a _____ of the legislature.

1.62 One of the governor's most awesome powers is the power to grant _____ and to commute sentences.

1.63 Normally the governor is the _____ of their political party.

1.64 The agency that distributes funds to the needy is the state _____ department.

1.65 The attorney general is the state's _____ .

1.66 Matters concerning the state's constitution are interpreted by the state _____ _____ .

1.67 The state's bills are paid by the state _____ .

1.68 The person in charge of the state's school system is the superintendent of public

_____ .

1.69 The state's funds are administered by the state _____ .

Judicial. The state court system is divided into local judicial districts. State judges may be either elected or appointed. The district attorney is the local prosecutor. Courts may be quite specialized within the district. Some courts may handle only criminal cases; others, only civil cases (lawsuits). Some may only handle divorces; others, only juvenile cases. Appeals from the district (or county) courts are handled by a state supreme court. Some states have what amounts to two supreme courts: one for civil cases (having to do with private individual property and rights), and the other for criminal cases.

The state supreme court may declare state laws unconstitutional. That is, they may declare them not in accord with the state constitution.

Appeals from the state supreme court go directly to the United States Supreme Court. The United States Supreme Court is the court of final appeal.

State officials (in whatever branch) have sworn to uphold both the federal and the state constitutions. State constitutions are similar to the national one (for example, they all have a bill of rights), but they tend to be much more complicated. The federal charter is a more general statement of principles, whereas the state constitution may be much more explicit. State constitutions are often amended. Sometimes the legislature has the power to pass amendments, but often the people must ratify all amendments in the general election. State constitutions may include everything from the pay of legislators to the length of the legislative session and to limits on state indebtedness.

Match the following.

1.70 _____ district attorney

1.71 _____ appeals

1.72 _____ final appeals

1.73 _____ state official

1.74 _____ state constitutions

a. United States Supreme Court

b. sworn to uphold state and federal constitutions

c. state supreme court

d. state archives

e. more explicit and complicated

f. local prosecutor

Review the material in this section in preparation for the Self Test. The Self Test will check your mastery of this particular section. The items missed on this Self Test will indicate specific areas where restudy is needed for mastery.

SELF TEST 1

Complete these sentences (each answer, 3 points).

1.01 The basic political unit in the United States is the _____ .

1.02 The Articles of Confederation were more of a(n) _____ than a government.

1.03 The a. _____ was part of an effort to

b. _____ the government under the Articles of Confederation.

1.04 The original purpose of the Constitutional Convention was to _____ the Articles.

1.05 Federal authority is _____ authority.

1.06 State governments possess a sovereignty _____ of the federal government.

1.07 The War of 1812 was opposed by several _____ states.

1.08 The doctrine of _____ means *the use of state sovereignty to block a federal law.*

1.09 Secession was no longer a choice for the states after the _____ .

1.010 The executive, the legislative, and the _____ are the three main divisions of state government.

1.011 In the executive branch of a state, the most important official is the _____ .

1.012 The state supreme court is part of the _____ branch.

1.013 Lord Acton wrote, "All _____ tends to corrupt, and absolute power corrupts absolutely."

1.014 The political thoughts of _____ provided theoretical justification for the United States system of checks and balances.

1.015 A legislature that has only one body is a(n) _____ legislature.

Answer true or false (each answer, 1 point).

1.016 _____ A unicameral legislature meets once a calendar year.

1.017 _____ The legislature may also be called the general assembly.

1.018 _____ The governor presides over the legislature.

1.019 _____ Legislators from a one-party state will mostly represent the dominant party.

1.020 _____ Liberals are those who most oppose Democratic Party programs.

1.021 _____ Many legislatures meet biennially.

1.022 _____ The governor may not veto a bill until it has already been approved by both houses of the legislature.

1.023 _____ Lobbyists represent special interest groups.

1.024 _____ The governor's power is immediate and uncontested.

1.025 _____ Long ballots assure strong governors.

1.026 _____ The attorney general represents the state in court.

1.027 _____ Appeals are heard by the state supreme court.

1.028 _____ The district attorney is a local prosecutor.

Match the following (each answer, 2 points).

1.029 _____ bicameral

1.030 _____ conservative

1.031 _____ checks and balances

1.032 _____ biennial

1.033 _____ House of Representatives

1.034 _____ speaker of the house

1.035 _____ liberal

1.036 _____ governor

1.037 _____ attorney general

1.038 _____ state archives

a. supports less government and balanced budgets

b. occurs every two years

c. controls the state police

d. place where state documents are kept

e. keep one branch of government from becoming too powerful

f. a state's lawyer

g. legislature with two houses

h. domination of an election by a group of voters

i. controls legislation and decides who may speak on the legislative floor

j. usually has about 100 members in most states

k. tend to favor more government

65 / 81

SCORE _____   TEACHER _____ _____

initials   date

2. STATE FINANCE

Finance concerns the way money is made and spent. Each state is responsible for financing certain projects, for paying salaries and debts, and for spending money in many other ways.

This section will cover the mechanics of state finance so that we may better understand the way in which a state handles its money.

SECTION OBJECTIVES

Review these objectives. When you have completed this section, you should be able to:

3. Discuss the significance of state spending.

4. Enumerate the types and meaning of state taxes.

5. Relate to taxes as a Christian citizen.

6. Explain and evaluate state borrowing.

VOCABULARY

Study this word to enhance your learning success in this section.

inflation (in flā′ shun). A rise in prices due to the amount of money in the economy growing faster than the amount of goods and services available.

SPENDING

State governments must spend a huge amount of money. The size of state budgets varies from state to state. New York and California—with their large populations and many state services—have much larger budgets and, therefore, expend more funds than smaller states such as Mississippi and New Hampshire.

State spending grows with the size of state government. The more government services that are provided, the higher state spending must be.

Much of the growth of state government has happened because of increases in the amount of state aid for public welfare and the growth of regulatory agencies. Much of the money spent by the welfare department comes from the federal government. Federal aid to the states can sometimes be expensive because federal funds must be matched by an equal amount from the state.

The large staffs required to distribute welfare funds are expensive. Office workers, administrators, and case workers must be employed in every part of the operation. Regulatory agencies require investigative staffs and even full-time attorneys. Legislative staffs also grow when lawmakers find the burden of research and correspondence too much to handle alone or with a very small staff.

The major expense of state government in recent years has been education. State governments support public education at all levels, from kindergarten to graduate school. Teachers' salaries, textbooks, buildings, and so forth must all be provided. A portion of the upkeep of every school district in the state comes from the state department of education. The rest of the money comes from local revenues or from grants-in-aid from the federal government.

State governments also spend large sums on highways, bridges, and roads. As with much state spending, some road projects are now partially or completely funded by the federal government. Other roads are built as toll roads, and motorists using them pay a fee until the road is paid for.

State governments are involved in other fields such as health (disease control, research, and education), agriculture, and conservation. States maintain agricultural research staffs and consultants called county agents. They also are involved with conservation projects (water, soil, and forest). They often employ people who research wildlife as well as those who police hunting and fishing (game wardens). States also maintain many natural forests and parks.

Another factor in total state spending is **inflation**. Inflation means that the amount of money in the economy is growing faster than the amount of goods and services available. The result is a rise in the prices of goods and services because money gets cheaper and cheaper. Salaries must be increased to keep up with rising prices.

In this situation the state government is a consumer like everyone else. It buys supplies, has buildings built, and hires workers. The state feels the pressure of inflation just as private businesses do.

The governor must consolidate and revise the budget requests of the state agencies and present a budget to the legislature each session. All funds used by the state must come from the legislature. If the legislature fails to give funds to an agency, the result would be the same as if the agency were legislated out of existence.

 Complete these activities.

2.1 Two states with the largest budgets are a. _____ and

b. _____ .

2.2 As state services rise, state spending _____ .

2.3 Federal aid can be expensive to the states because each dollar given must be

_____ by the state.

2.4 Growth of state government has been caused, in part, by the increase in public

_____ .

2.5 The major expense of state government is for _____ .

2.6 A sudden rise in prices caused by the amount of money in the economy growing faster than

the amount of goods and services available is called _____ .

2.7 Who submits a state budget to the legislature? _____

2.8 Who appropriates state funds? _____

2.9 The state government buying supplies is a _____ like everyone else.

2.10 Projects involving water, soil, and forests are called _____ projects.

HISTORY & GEOGRAPHY 709

LIFEPAC TEST

NAME _____

DATE _____

SCORE _____

HISTORY & GEOGRAPHY 709: LIFEPAC TEST

Match the terms (each answer, 2 points).

1. _____ bicameral
2. _____ governor
3. _____ precinct
4. _____ progressive tax
5. _____ liberal
6. _____ Proposition 13
7. _____ inflation
8. _____ speaker
9. _____ attorney general
10. _____ utility

a. gas or telephone company
b. increases as income increases
c. ended the Civil War
d. basic geographical voting area
e. favors more government
f. controls state police
g. presides over a house of representatives
h. a state's lawyer
i. rapid rise in prices
j. having two legislative houses
k. taxpayers' revolt measure in California

Complete these sentences using these terms (each answer, 3 points).

Republican	district attorney	power	lobbyist
judicial	taxpayer	match	conservation
Democratic	education	income	

11. Lord Acton said, "All _____ tends to corrupt, and absolute power corrupts absolutely."

12. Taxes upon the money people earn from jobs or investments are called _____ taxes.

13. When the federal government gives money to a state, the state is often required to _____ each dollar with a dollar of its own.

14. A person who represents a special interest group is called a _____ .

15. A local prosecutor is called a _____ .

16. A Christian citizen should be a willing _____ .

17. More money from a state's treasury is spent every year on _____ than any other item.

18. The three branches of state government are the executive, the legislative, and the

    _____ .

19. The political party that was in control of the Presidency for the majority of the years from

    1932 to 1996 was the _____ Party.

20. Projects involving water, soil, and forests are called _____ projects.

Answer true or false (each answer, 1 point).

21. _____ Primary elections are held to choose candidates.

22. _____ A sales tax is a progressive tax.

23. _____ Jesus said to give everything to Caesar.

24. _____ In state legislatures the House is larger than the Senate.

25. _____ All states have a governor.

26. _____ All state legislatures have two parts.

27. _____ A political conservative probably favors a balanced budget.

28. _____ The attorney general is the state's chief executive.

29. _____ A unicameral legislature meets once a year.

30. _____ The Christian must make decisions about politics based on the Word of God.

Write the letter for the correct answer on each line (each answer, 3 points).

31. Taxes on the value of property one inherits are called _____ .
    a. inheritance taxes   b. estate taxes   c. death taxes   d. sales taxes

32. The official who must present a budget to the state legislature is the _____ .
    a. governor   b. secretary of state c. treasurer   d. auditor

33. The American political tradition originated in _____ .
    a. Canada   b. Africa   c. Germany   d. England

34. A group of people who organize to nominate and elect certain candidates is a _____ .
    a. labor union   b. precinct convention
    c. protest march   d. political party

TAXING

Traditionally, state funds have come from taxes—many still do. They are not the chief source of funds, however. More funds come from federal grants than from any other source. A tax is a charge to an individual or corporation levied by the government. It is never optional. It must be paid.

Property tax. One of the principal sources of state revenue is the property tax. Although these taxes are normally collected by local authorities, a portion of the taxes collected goes to the state. Property taxes are charged to the *assessed value* of a piece of property. A home may be sold on the market at a price far higher than its assessed value. In fact, *market value* is normally higher than assessed value.

In recent years, local and state governments have been raising property tax rates as well as raising assessed values to more closely resemble market values. Such changes have severely damaged the pocketbooks of many elderly people and other low-income families. A couple may have spent years paying off a loan on their house, but now they are unable to afford to pay their taxes. In some cases two years' taxes total the original purchase price of the home.

Such abuses are what caused the people of California and several other states to launch a "taxpayers' revolt" in the 1970's. In California, voters passed Proposition 13, which called for a drastic reduction in state taxes and changes in methods of valuing property. In recent years, politicians running for every office from county commissioner to United States senator were talking about reducing taxes. Taxes and government spending have grown together. Many people believe that the percentage of the United States gross national product now spent on government is entirely too high.

Property taxes are usually collected by local governments (cities, counties, and school districts), and a percentage of the locally collected taxes is then sent to the state. Many local school systems are funded by property taxes. Many judges and others concerned with the funding of education have objected to what they consider an inequality in the funding of public education.

In a poor area where land values are low, school tax revenues are necessarily lower. In a rich suburban school district, tax revenues are normally much greater. Obviously, a school district

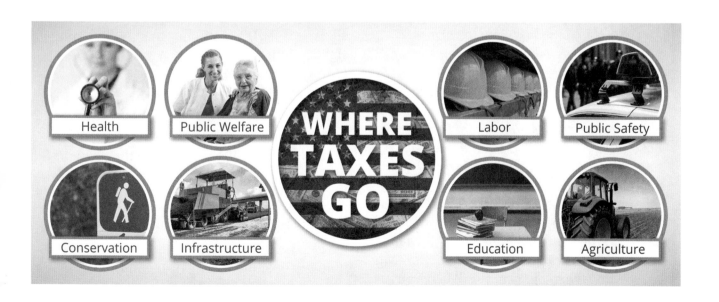

in a suburb composed of well-to-do executives and their families has more money to spend than a district in a poorer rural area. Those who object to this procedure would like for all the tax monies to be placed in a common pot and then redistributed to local areas on a more equal basis. Their assumption is that inequalities resulting from wealth are wrong. Others would say that such inequalities and the opportunity through self-betterment to move into the more wealthy class is simply the essence of freedom and the free enterprise system. The government (state, local, and federal) has the power and the right to tax. This right is not only Biblical, but it is also a sovereign right of government. A government without the power to tax would be no government at all. The government has the power to tax, and it has the power to use force in the collection of taxes.

Government is by definition organized force. The government was designed by God to be a protector of the whole society. Man has the right to police himself, but God alone is the possessor of inherent sovereignty. He alone possesses an authority that does not come from another source. The authority of government comes from God. Likewise, the government's authority to tax comes from God.

In Romans 13:1 through 6, Paul exhorted his fellow-believers to be subject to "the higher powers":

> Let every soul be subject unto the higher powers. For there is no power but of God: the powers that be are ordained of God. Whosoever therefore resisteth the power, resisteth the ordinance of God: and they that resist shall receive to themselves damnation. For rulers are not a terror to good works, but to the evil. Wilt thou then not be afraid of the power? Do that which is good, and thou shalt have praise of the same: For he is the minister of God to thee for good. But if thou do that which is evil, be afraid; for he beareth not the sword in vain: for he is the minister of God, a revenger to execute wrath upon him that doeth evil. Wherefore ye

> must needs be subject, not only for wrath, but also for conscience sake. For this cause pay ye tribute also: for they are God's ministers, attending continually upon this very thing.

In Romans 13:6 Paul mentions the taxing power of the government, "For this cause pay ye tribute also: For they are God's ministers, attending continually upon this very thing."

The word *tribute* in this passage means *taxes*. The government's right to levy taxes is Biblical. The Christian citizen is to be a taxpayer. Even Jesus recognized the government's authority to levy taxes. Jesus, the Lord of the universe, paid a tax to Caesar, the Roman emperor. Jesus said upon that occasion (Mark 12:17), "Render to Caesar the things that are Caesar's, and to God the things that are God's..." Some things are proper for government, but other things belong to God. Those activities and laws that belong to government must be supported by the follower of Christ.

To the question, "Should the government ever be disobeyed?" the answer is "yes." The government may be disobeyed but only when it attempts to control "those things that are God's." Peter and the other Apostles faced this dilemma in Jerusalem before the Sanhedrin. This council of Jewish elders called Peter and John before it (Acts 4:18) and "...commanded them not to speak at all nor teach in the name of Jesus." In reply, the two Apostles of Christ said (Acts 4:19), "...Whether it be right in the sight of God to hearken unto you more than unto God, judge ye."

After they had left the council, Peter and John continued to preach and teach in the name of Jesus. Upon a subsequent arrest the council asked Peter and the others why they had disobeyed. Peter replied (Acts 5:29),"... We ought to obey God rather than men." When a government says we may not preach the Gospel, we must disobey because our commission is clear: we are to teach all nations. In which other area of ministry or life this principle may apply is a matter for godly, individual decisions.

Complete these activities.

2.11 The taxable value of property is the _____ value.

2.12 What property can be sold for is the _____ value.

2.13 A charge on individuals and corporations to raise money for the government is called a _____ .

2.14 Proposition 13 was a revolt against state taxes and property taxes in _____ .

2.15 Property taxes are collected by the _____ government.

2.16 When one area of a state is poorer than another, its children usually get a poorer

_____ .

2.17 From whom does the government derive its authority? _____

2.18 Government was designed by God to be a(n) _____ of the whole society.

2.19 Should a Christian citizen be a taxpayer? _____

2.20 What did Jesus tell his disciples about taxes? _____

_____

Income tax. Income tax is a tax upon the money people earn from jobs or investments. State income tax on an individual is normally a *progressive tax*: that is, the tax increases as income increases. State income taxes do not rise as steeply as federal taxes do. The tax rate on corporations is usually a flat rate. Progressive taxes are said to benefit the poor at the expense of the rich. Some students of taxation, however, believe that progressive income taxes destroy the incentive to produce more or to make more money.

Sales tax. Sales taxes are taxes based on the sales prices of merchandise. An item may have the retail price of $1.00, but a 5 percent sales tax is added so that the customer must pay $1.05 with the extra $.05 going to the government. Many people believe that a sales tax is a *regressive tax* because it taxes everyone the same whatever their income is. They believe that such a tax penalizes the poor. In other words, the person who makes $12,000 per year will be hurt more by having to pay an additional five cents

on every dollar than the person who makes $35,000 per year. The first person simply has less money to begin with.

Usually those who support sales taxes reply that the government should not charge any more to one citizen than it does to another, because the wealth one accumulates has nothing to do with the government, and that the rich man will pay more because he buys more.

Most people who oppose the state sales tax are those who are in favor of state income taxes. They prefer a tax that penalizes those with more wealth. Conservatives tend to favor sales taxes; people who are more liberal tend to prefer progressive income taxes.

Nobody who pays taxes really likes either approach. Because of the possible inequities to the poor of sales taxes, many states do not tax such goods as groceries and prescription drugs because they are necessities. Many states also do not tax services (such as banks and dentists).

Inheritance · Estate · TYPES of TAXES · Excise · Income · Sales · Severance · Property · Licensing

Other taxes. Other types of taxes include *excise taxes*, those taxes charged for specific items such as gasoline. Another kind of tax charged by the state is the fee for a license on the right to do something, such as hunt, fish, drive, boat, get married, or own a dog. States also charge franchise taxes on the right to run a business or a public utility. Some states also charge inheritance or estate taxes. *Inheritance taxes* are charged on the value of the property an individual inherits from someone who died. *Estate taxes* are charged to the estate before it is divided among the heirs. States also levy taxes called *severance* taxes upon natural resources that are taken from the ground (oil, coal, timber, and so forth).

Many different taxes are levied by state governments. Many of these taxes fall on business. One main question about taxation is always who bears the burden of a tax. The burden of a tax if often termed its *incidence.* Often a business will include taxes in the price of its product.

In such cases, the incidence of taxation is said to shift, and the consumer pays the tax. Shifting the incidence of taxation is especially practiced by governmentally- protected monopolies, such as utilities. (A monopoly is a business with no close competition.)

Taxes have been on the rise in the twentieth century. The Bureau of Statistics has released figures that indicate sharp increases in the rate of total taxes: federal, state, and local. In 1902, the total taxes paid in the United States amounted to only $1.4 billion. By 1984 the total had risen to $735.0 billion. State and local taxes have risen from roughly $10 billion in 1940 to $141.5 billion in 1975. State taxes exceeded federal taxes until about 1940. Now federal tax dollars account for significantly more than all state and local government taxes put together.

Write the letter for the correct answer on each line.

2.21 Taxes upon the money people earn are _____ .
a. sales taxes   b. income taxes   c. severance taxes   d. excise taxes

2.22 A tax in which those with higher incomes pay a higher rate is a _____ .
a. generated tax   b. regressive tax   c. theological tax   d. progressive tax

2.23 Some students of taxation believe that progressive taxes destroy the _____ .
a. incentive to produce more   b. machinery to produce more
c. duty to produce more

2.24 Taxes on the price of merchandise are _____ .
a. estate taxes   b. franchise taxes   c. sales taxes   d. income taxes

2.25 Many believe that the sales tax is a _____ .
a. progressive tax   b. motivated tax   c. inspirational tax   d. regressive tax

2.26 Politicians who tend to favor sales taxes as opposed to income taxes are more _____ .
a. conservative   b. liberal   c. candid

2.27 Taxes on specific items are called _____ .
a. franchise taxes   b. license taxes   c. excise taxes

2.28 Taxes on the value of a property one inherits are called _____ .
a. inheritance taxes   b. estate taxes   c. death taxes

2.29 Taxes upon the use of natural resources are called _____ .
a. estate taxes   b. severance taxes   c. excise taxes

2.30 The burden of taxation is termed the _____ .
a. frequency of taxation   b. incidence of taxation
c. meaning of taxation

2.31 Shifting the incidence of a tax is often done by _____ .
a. shoe shops   b. monopolies   c. corporations

2.32 Total taxes in 1902 were about _____ .
a. $1.4 billion   b. $2 billion   c. $3.5 billion

2.33 Today the total dollars of state and local taxes are _____ .
a. the same as federal taxes   b. less than federal taxes
c. more than federal taxes

BORROWING

Until recently, state debts were small. Now, increased spending has caused some states to go heavily into debt. The debts of a state must be paid out of the money it collects. Most state constitutions have limits on the amount of long-term debts a state may have.

Most states require that the voters approve any issue of long-term bonds. A bond is a certificate that is issued for a certain amount that matures (after a specified period at a specified rate called the face amount). Many bonds may be bought and sold on the open market. The market price may be quite different from the face value of the bond.

States use several different types of bonds. *Serial bonds* are issued in series and some of them pay off each year. *General obligation bonds* are supported by the credit of the issuing government. *Revenue bonds* are backed by the income a certain project produces.

State governments also have *short-term debts.* These debts pay for such emergencies as employees' salaries when not enough money is otherwise available. Examples of short-term debts are bank loans, tax anticipation warrants, and other notes.

State governments receive many grants (gifts) from the United States government as part of "revenue sharing." Thirty billion dollars has been given to the states in this way.

In revenue sharing, the federal government through its broader tax base distributes money at local levels where the needs exist. This procedure has not always worked, since the federal government often attaches conditions to its gifts. These extra requirements are often resented at the state level.

Complete these activities.

2.34 _____ debt is often limited by state constitutions.

2.35 A _____ is a certificate that is issued for a certain amount that matures.

2.36 Bank loans, tax anticipation warrants, and other notes are _____ -term debts.

2.37 _____ sharing is collecting taxes at the federal level and distributing them at the local level.

2.38 List three kinds of bonds.

a. _____   b. _____

c. _____

Complete this activity.

2.39 Think about the situation Peter and the Apostles found themselves in. Write a 200-word essay describing and analyzing the question "Should a Christian ever disobey the government and if so, when?"

TEACHER CHECK _____ _____
                        initials   date

Review the material in this section in preparation for the Self Test. This Self Test will check your mastery of this particular section as well as your knowledge of the previous section.

SELF TEST 2

Match the terms (each answer, 2 points).

2.01	_____ state	a.	federal authority
2.02	_____ bicameral	b.	local prosecutor
2.03	_____ appeals	c.	used by New England states in 1814
2.04	_____ lobbyists	d.	chief executive
2.05	_____ derived	e.	checks and balances
2.06	_____ governor	f.	basic political unit
2.07	_____ district attorney	g.	special interest groups
2.08	_____ Civil War	h.	market price
2.09	_____ interposition	i.	state supreme court
2.010	_____ Montesquieu	j.	two houses
		k.	forced an end to secession

Write the letter for the correct answer on each line (each answer, 3 points).

2.011 The more state services that are provided, the higher state _____ .
a. politics will be   b. spending will be   c. religion will be

2.012 The major expense of state governments is _____ .
a. education   b. parks and recreation
c. the governor's staff

2.013 The situation in which the amount of available money increases faster than the amount of available goods is known as _____ .
a. racing   b. poverty   c. inflation   d. politics

2.014 The official who must present a budget to the legislature is the _____ .
a. governor   b. secretary of state   c. treasurer   d. auditor

2.015 A piece of property is taxed at its _____ .
a. market value   b. assessed value   c. real value

2.016 A charge levied for the support of the government is a _____ .
a. fine   b. tax   c. price

2.017 Most state money comes from _____ .
a. taxes   b. federal grants   c. speeding tickets

2.018 Elderly people are especially hurt by increases in _____ .
a. property taxes   b. income taxes   c. sales taxes

2.019 Property taxes are collected by the _____ .
a. state government b. federal government
c. local government

2.020 A sovereign right of government is the power to _____ .
a. tax   b. legislate   c. license

Complete these sentences (each answer, 3 points).

2.021 Only God possesses inherent _____ .

2.022 Government is defined as organized _____ .

2.023 The government's authority comes from _____ .

2.024 According to the Bible, the Christian citizen should be a _____ payer.

2.025 Jesus said to render to Caesar the things that are _____ .

2.026 Taxes upon earnings are _____ taxes.

2.027 A progressive tax is one in which those with higher incomes pay a _____ rate.

2.028 The sales tax is regarded by some people as _____ .

2.029 Some people believed that progressive taxes destroy the _____ to produce.

2.030 Conservatives tend to favor _____ taxes over income taxes.

Match the terms (each answer, 2 points).

2.031	_____ excise tax	a. burden
2.032	_____ incidence	b. paid by beneficiary of a will
2.033	_____ severance	c. constitutional limits
2.034	_____ inheritance tax	d. bank loan
2.035	_____ long-term debt	e. inherent sovereignty
2.036	_____ short-term debt	f. price increases
2.037	_____ God	g. tax revolt
2.038	_____ inflation	h. use of natural resources
2.039	_____ appropriates	i. paid on specified items
2.040	_____ education	j. major expense
		k. legislature

80 / 100   SCORE _____   TEACHER _____ _____
initials   date

3. STATE POLITICS

Two sides exist for every question. In government some people want more, others less.

Thus political parties have arisen. In this section we shall discuss how political parties operate.

SECTION OBJECTIVES

Review these objectives. When you have completed this section, you should be able to:

7. Describe state political parties.

8. Differentiate between liberals and conservatives.

9. Discuss the elements of political power.

VOCABULARY

Study these words to enhance your learning success in this section.

humanist (hyü' mu nist). A person concerned with human interests or values.

mercantilism (mer' kun ti liz um). An economic system in Europe in the eighteenth century.

platform (plat' form). In politics, a plan of action or statement of the beliefs of a group.

precinct (prē' singkt). A part or district within a city.

primary election (prī' mer ē i lek' shun). An election to choose candidates for office from a certain political party.

POLITICAL PARTIES

The role of political parties varies from state to state. In some states both major parties are important. In others, one party is dominant, and most if not all state-level officials are from the dominant party. Minor parties play different roles from state to state. In New York, the *Liberal Party* is a significant influence upon the Democratic Party; its counterpart, the *Conservative Party*, is an influence upon the Republicans.

Although there are hundreds of political parties in the United States, only a few are able to have candidates on election ballots. In 1972 the *Liberation Party*, which wants almost no government at all, ran a national presidential campaign. Some third-party movements have appeared briefly. In 1948 several Southern states were actually carried by the *States' Rights*, or *Dixiecrat Party*, candidate for president,

Strom Thurmond of South Carolina. Another Southerner, George Wallace, ran a strong race for president as a candidate of the *American Independence Party* in 1968. In the 1990's Ross Perot ran in repeated presidential elections as a candidate for the Reform Party he created.

A *political party* is a group of voters organized to support candidates who espouse the beliefs of the group as a whole. Political parties exist in almost every country on earth. They can even be found in monarchies and dictatorships, sometimes as part of a revolutionary movement. The United States is one of the few democratic countries whose politics are dominated by only two parties. European countries have many strong political parties.

History. American political parties reflect a tradition that began in England. England in the eighteenth century had developed two dominant parties, the *Whigs* and the *Tories.* (The Tories still exist today but are known as the *Conservatives.* The Whigs are known as the *Liberal Party*, but their membership in Parliament has dwindled during this century as the socialist *Labour Party* has gained in membership.) The Tories were the party of the aristocracy. They favored the landowning nobility, the established church, the House of Lords, **mercantilism**, and tradition. The Whigs tended to be the party of the rising middle class industrialists, of the House of Commons, of capitalism, of free trade, and later of political and social reform.

The English colonies reflected the political divisions of England. Normally the royal governor and his supporters were Tories. The views were those of the English nobility in general. Many colonists were not impressed with the nobility in England and disliked its traditional ideas. They had left England in the first place because of the restrictions placed on them by the English ruling class and the established church. Politically they were Whigs. Such party divisions occurred in the colonial popular assemblies.

At the time of the American Revolution, those who remained loyal to the British government were called Tories. Those who joined the revolution were known as Whigs. The Whigs were not all alike, of course. John Adams was much more conservative than his rabble-rousing cousin, Samuel Adams. Thomas Jefferson was more of a libertarian than his fellow Virginian, George Washington.

When the United States government first met under President Washington, party organizations had not yet been formed. Washington and most of the other advocates of the new Constitution had become known as "Federalists." The party that eventually organized under that name, however, is more closely linked to Alexander Hamilton, the first secretary of the treasury.

Hamilton tended to favor the rising merchant-industrial interests of the Northeast. He and his followers wanted a sound currency and financial system, a strong central government, and closer ties with the British. Hamilton openly clashed with Washington's secretary of state, Thomas Jefferson, who favored a weak central government, states' rights, a liberal view of racial equality, and closer relations with France.

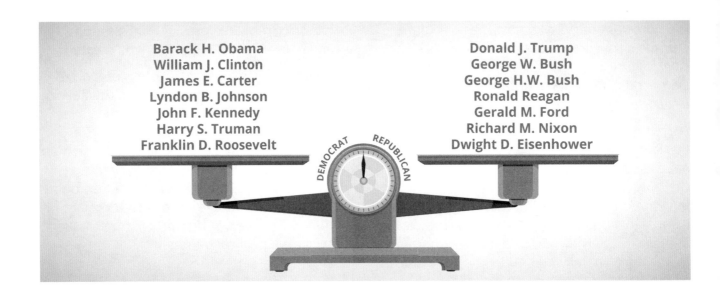

Barack H. Obama
William J. Clinton
James E. Carter
Lyndon B. Johnson
John F. Kennedy
Harry S. Truman
Franklin D. Roosevelt

DEMOCRAT   REPUBLICAN

Donald J. Trump
George W. Bush
George H.W. Bush
Ronald Reagan
Gerald M. Ford
Richard M. Nixon
Dwight D. Eisenhower

Jefferson believed in a strict construction of the Constitution. A party organization developed around Jefferson's beliefs. Jefferson's party became known as the *Democratic-Republicans.* This party still exists as the Democratic Party.

Federalists were strongest in the South. The middle states were less decisive. The only president who was a member of the Federalist Party was John Adams. For several years the only effective political party was the Democratic-Republicans. The only Federalists were left in the New England states. Many men with Federalist views, such as James Madison and John Quincy Adams, joined the Democratic-Republicans.

After Andrew Jackson became president, Democrats who opposed him split to form the *National Republican Party*. In 1832 many National Republicans joined with conservatives from the Democrats as well as former Federalists to form the Whig Party. Among important Whigs were Henry Clay, John Quincy Adams, and Daniel Webster. The Whig Party tended to support industry, protective tariffs, and the Union. The party was divided on the slavery issue, however. In the late 1850's many northern Whigs joined the new anti-slavery *Republican Party.* Southerners tended to rejoin the Democrats. The Republicans elected Abraham Lincoln president in 1860.

The Republicans dominated northern politics for most of the years that followed the Civil War. The South became more heavily Democratic. The Democrats only elected two men to the Presidency between 1860 and 1933, Grover Cleveland and Woodrow Wilson.

In the years after President Franklin Roosevelt took office, the Democrats once again became the majority party. The Republicans have held the White House for only twenty-eight years since 1932 and had controlled Congress only eight years, during the years 1947 to 1949; 1953 to 1955; and 1994 to 1998.

The Republican Party today carries on the tradition of the Federalists and Whigs. It tends to support business interests, sound money, less international involvement, and less government. Many Democrats, especially in the South, still support a strong states' rights view, but the Democrats in general have become a more big-government party. They have tended to support increased federal spending, more government involvement in the economy, and more social legislation.

Interestingly, the Democrats have been the party that was in power throughout most of the major wars of this century involving the United States: World War I (Wilson), World War II (Franklin Roosevelt), the Korean War (Truman), and Vietnam (Kennedy and Johnson). Republicans with their conservative economic policies have witnessed several economic slumps during their administrations.

Party politics is now in a process of change in the United States. The Midwest is no longer solidly Republican. The South is not so solidly Democratic. In 1978 both Texas and Tennessee elected their first Republican governors since Reconstruction. Such states as Iowa and Illinois are capable of sending liberal Democrats as well as Republicans to Congress or even the Senate. Republicans are now members of state legislatures in such previously Democratic strongholds as Mississippi and Florida.

Complete the vocabulary crossword.

3.1   **ACROSS**
1. A person concerned with human interests or values.
2. An economic system in Europe in the eighteenth century.
3. In politics, a plan of action or statement of the beliefs of a group.

DOWN
4. A sudden rise in prices caused by the amount of money in the economy growing faster than the amount of goods and services available.
5. A part or district within a city.
6. An election to choose candidates for office from a certain political party.

Complete these sentences.

3.2   The role of political parties _____ from state to state.

3.3   In New York the a. _____ Party tends to influence the Democrats, and the

b. _____ Party tends to influence the Republicans.

3.4   The Reform Party presidential candidate in the 1990s was _____ .

3.5 A group of voters who organize to support political candidates who share their beliefs is called a _____ .

3.6 American political parties reflect a tradition that originated in _____ .

3.7 In early America a. _____ were the party of the nobility, and

b. _____ were the party of the middle class.

3.8 The royal governor and his supporters tended to be _____ .

3.9 At the time of the American Revolution, the _____ were those who remained loyal to England.

3.10 The first major federalist leader was Alexander _____ .

3.11 Jefferson's views were espoused by the _____ Party.

3.12 The anti-Jackson Democrats favored the National _____ Party.

3.13 In 1832 several groups merged into the _____ Party.

3.14 Two famous Whigs were Henry a. _____ and Daniel b. _____ .

3.15 The dominant party in the United States from 1860 to 1933 was the _____ Party.

3.16 The only Democratic presidents between 1860 and 1933 were a. _____ and

b. _____ .

3.17 The Republicans have only controlled Congress for _____ of the years between 1932 and 1998.

3.18 The Federalists, the _____ , and the Republicans are all in the same political tradition.

3.19 Democrats today tend to favor more _____ involvement in the economy.

Organization. Political parties are organized at the **precinct**, county, state, and national levels. Even at the national level, however, the states are represented as states. Members of the national committee of a party serve as state representatives, not as individuals. National conventions poll the delegates state by state.

Party organization begins at the precinct level. A precinct is a geographical voting area. Each party tries to have a chairman and a committee in every voting precinct throughout the state. Each precinct holds a *precinct convention*, usually following the party **primary election** (a popular election of party nominees). The precinct convention passes a precinct **platform** and nominates delegates to the county convention. The county convention elects delegates to the state convention and passes a county platform. The same process is repeated at the state level. Some small parties even nominate state and local candidates in these conventions, but major parties usually hold party primaries. The party's primary is an election to determine who the party's candidates will be in the general election. If no candidate for nomination receives a clear majority, normally a run off election is held a month later.

States are now using *presidential preferential primaries* as a means of telling which slate of delegates should attend the national convention. Some states allow citizens to *cross-ballot,* to vote for some candidates of both parties. In some states the primary has really been the election since the opposing parties have been unable to get their candidates elected, especially for state and local officials.

Each state party has a chairman who is the administrator of the party and heads an administrative staff, and an executive committee to set policy between conventions. The chairman is usually the chief propaganda voice of the party. The official leader of the party is usually the governor or some other high elected official.

Sometimes a group within the party becomes dissatisfied and holds a *rump,* or unofficial, convention of its own. Often they elect their own delegates to the national convention. The national committee then has to determine which delegates are official and may be seated.

Complete this activity.

3.20 List four levels of party organization.

a. _____   b. _____

c. _____   d. _____

Complete these sentences.

3.21 Political party organization begins at the _____ level.

3.22 A popular election of party nominees is called a _____ election.

3.23 A county convention elects delegates to the _____ convention.

3.24 A geographical voting area is called a _____ .

3.25 Cross balloting means voting for candidates of both _____ .

3.26 A means of telling which state delegates should attend the national convention is a preferential _____ .

3.27 The person who administers a political party and heads the administrative staff is the party _____ .

3.28 An unofficial convention held by a dissatisfied faction within a party is called a _____ convention.

VIEWPOINTS

Two major viewpoints in both state and national politics are *liberalism* and *conservatism.* Strangely enough, the historical use of these two terms is not quite the same as that used today in the United States.

Originally, conservatives were the advocates of royalty-established (state-controlled) churches, and the nobility. Liberals were believers in the free market, less centralized authority, and more individual freedoms. At the time of the drafting of the Constitution, conservatives such as Hamilton argued for a strong central government. Thomas Jefferson, considered a liberal and an enlightened **humanist**, opposed strong central governments and supported states' rights.

During the middle and late nineteenth century, liberals began to support progressive social legislation of various types and social equality and material prosperity for the masses. Today the term liberal tends to mean those who favor more government involvement in society. Instead of a relatively free market, liberals have called for government intervention in business and sometimes outright socialism.

Conservatism today encompasses many varied groups. One group favors a much stronger free enterprise system and little or no government interference in the economy. Old-fashioned conservatives of the Alexander Hamilton type favor increased law and order. The traditional conservative is generally more religious than the libertarian conservative.

In politics the differences within conservatism as well as those within liberalism (which includes populism, a kind of rural, nationalistic socialism, and sophisticated international government advocates) are not so great as they often appear. Sometimes populists who are really socialists are classed as conservatives because of their social views.

Sometimes liberals and conservatives are divided along party lines: the liberals are Democrats; the conservatives are Republicans. In some areas this statement is not true, however. Many northeastern Republicans are liberals. Southern Democrats are often very conservative. In fact, some states are so dominated by one party that often conservative and liberal factions within the party have more significance at the state level than party labels do.

Many people prefer not to be called either conservative or liberal. They are usually called moderates.

Moderates would rather deal with problems and issues as they arise on the basis of what seems to work best rather than on the basis of an existing set of principles. They reflect another *tradition,* that of pragmatism. According to pragmatic thinkers, what is *important* is what *works.* Many politicians find pragmatism

| Thomas Jefferson

convenient because political decisions require many compromises. The obvious difficulty is that some objective standards of right and wrong are needed even in political decisions.

The Christian in politics is in a unique position. Christians are not bound by any of man's philosophies of government, yet they are not pragmatist. They must make decisions based upon the written Word of God (the Bible) and under the leadership of the Holy Spirit. A

number of individuals in political office today are professing believers in Christ. They may be found in almost every political camp. Keeping abreast of current affairs will often provide valuable insight into their political and personal beliefs. These office-holders are under a tremendous amount of pressure due to the nature of politics. They need the prayerful support of fellow Christians throughout the United States.

Complete this activity.

3.29 Name the two predominant political viewpoints.

a. _____   b. _____

Complete these sentences.

3.30 Those who favored royalty, the established church, and the nobility were the original

_____ .

3.31 Those who believed in the free market, less centralized authority and more individual

freedom were the original _____ .

3.32 A supporter of strong central government was Alexander a. _____ ; in

favor of weak central government and states rights' was Thomas b. _____ .

3.33 In the late nineteenth century _____ began to support social legislation,

social equality, and material prosperity for the masses.

3.34 Many modern conservatives favor little or no interference from the _____ .

3.35 The Christian in politics must make decisions based upon the _____ .

3.36 Populism is a kind of rural, nationalistic _____ .

3.37 Populists are sometimes classed as conservatives because of their stands on _____

views.

3.38 People who are pragmatists and deal with problems on the basis of what works are often

called _____ .

3.39 Pragmatism is convenient to many politicians because politics requires many

_____ .

3.40 The believing politician is in a _____ position.

POWER

Politics is a game of power. All men and women who enter the political arena seek power for one reason or another. Some wish to do good for their fellow men. Others wish only to help themselves and their friends to more wealth. Those who wish to do good may abuse power by using it to browbeat anyone who opposes their ideas.

A Christian may desire power because they believe that they can testify for Christ and can apply the Gospel to social or governmental issues. Even the believer, however, must be careful not to abuse power.

Within state boundaries many political machines have flourished. A *political machine* is dedicated to electing and keeping in office a certain group of candidates. It wants a monopoly of all the office-holders within the state. It does not welcome competition. Tammany Hall of New York City was a powerful group of New York Democrats. It controlled the city of New York for many years and was influential in state politics throughout the 19th and early 20th centuries. Like other political machines, they were associated with scandals and corruption.

In the South, political machines have been established with various families: the Byrds of Virginia, the Talmadges of Georgia, the Longs of Louisiana, and others. Texas politics was dominated for many years by Sam Rayburn, who was Speaker of the House, and also by Lyndon Johnson, who became president.

Republican politics has been dominated by men of finance and business. The Rockefellers of New York are examples of this kind of influence. Corporate executives and professional people are sources of Republican votes and money.

Labor unions have also been sources of political power. The AFL-CIO attempts to influence candidates through its Committee on Political Education (COPE). Business interests, such as oil and gas companies and insurance companies, also try to influence politics. The main tool all of these groups use is money. Candidates need money to win, and the unions and corporations have the money. The problems come when these groups try to buy or to bribe the candidate for jobs or for legislation.

Abuses of political power do not always go unprotested. Often a candidate will arise who will not cooperate with the machine. They may even oppose it. Such a person is called a *reform candidate.* Fiorello La Guardia won the mayorship of New York City away from Tammany Hall as a reform candidate.

Complete these sentences.

3.41 Politics is a game of _____ .

3.42 A Christian may desire power to testify for Christ and apply the _____ to social issues.

3.43 Even a Christian must be careful not to _____ power.

3.44 An organization dedicated to electing and keeping in office a certain group of candidates is a political _____ .

3.45 New York Democrats have often been controlled by _____ Hall.

3.46 Texas politics was once dominated by Sam _____ and Lyndon _____ .

3.47 A political machine does not welcome _____ .

3.48 Republicans tend to be dominated by men of _____ and _____ .

3.49 The _____ tries to influence men and legislation through its Committee on Political Education.

3.50 The main tool of those who seek political influence is _____ .

3.51 A candidate who opposes the machine is a _____ candidate.

Before you take this last Self Test, you may want to do one or more of these self checks.

1. _____ Read the objectives. See if you can do them.
2. _____ Restudy the material related to any objectives that you cannot do.
3. _____ Use the **SQ3R** study procedure to review the material:
   a. **S**can the sections.
   b. **Q**uestion yourself.
   c. **R**ead to answer your questions.
   d. **R**ecite the answers to yourself.
   e. **R**eview areas you did not understand.
4. _____ Review all vocabulary, activities, and Self Tests, writing a correct answer for every wrong answer.

SELF TEST 3

Match the following (each answer, 2 points).

3.01	_____ two houses	a.	local prosecutor
3.02	_____ Civil War	b.	too many dollars
3.03	_____ special interest groups	c.	income tax
3.04	_____ education	d.	bicameral
3.05	_____ inflation	e.	inherent authority
3.06	_____ governor	f.	lobbyists
3.07	_____ God	g.	forced an end to secession
3.08	_____ progressive	h.	major expense of the state
3.09	_____ tax	i.	presents budget to legislature
3.010	_____ district attorney	j.	specific terms
		k.	a sovereign right

Write the letter for the correct answer on each line (each answer, 3 points).

3.011 The role of political parties from state to state _____ .
a. varies   b. is the same   c. does not change

3.012 The party in New York that tends to influence the Republican Party is the _____ .
a. Liberal party   b. Dixiecrat party   c. Conservative party

3.013 A group of people who organize to nominate and elect certain candidates is a _____ .
a. political party   b. special interest group
c. labor union

3.014 The United states political tradition originated in _____ .
a. Canada   b. Austria   c. England

3.015 The party of the nobility were the _____ .
a. Whigs   b. Marxists   c. Tories

3.016 At the time of the American Revolution, those who supported independence were the_____ .
a. Tories   b. British   c. Whigs   d. Americans

3.017 The Federalists have the same political tradition as the Whigs and the _____ .
a. Republicans   b. Democrats   c. Dixiecrats

3.018 Henry Clay was a famous _____ .
a. Federalist   b. Whig   c. Democrat

3.019 The oldest American political party is the _____ .
a. Democrat Party   b. Republican Party   c. Libertarian Party

3.020 The basic local party organization is the _____ .
a. county   b. precinct   c. state

Complete these sentences (each answer, 3 points).

3.021 Party candidates are nominated by means of a party _____ election.

3.022 Voting in the primaries for both major parties is called _____ voting.

3.023 A dissatisfied group within the party will sometimes hold a _____ convention.

3.024 The two predominant political viewpoints are _____ and conservatism.

3.025 Liberals of today want more _____ involvement on the economy.

3.026 Liberals used to want most _____ enterprise.

3.027 The sales tax is regarded by some people as _____ .

3.028 Moderates reflect the philosophy of _____ .

3.029 Politics is a struggle for _____ .

3.030 Political power is often controlled by political _____ which want a monopoly of all the office holders in a state.

Before taking the LIFEPAC Test, you may want to do one or more of these self checks.

1. _____ Read the objectives. See if you can do them.
2. _____ Restudy the material related to any objectives that you cannot do.
3. _____ Use the **SQ3R** study procedure to review the material.
4. _____ Review activities, Self Tests, and LIFEPAC vocabulary words.
5. _____ Restudy areas of weakness indicated by the last Self Test.